CIRCUS

CIRCUS

DANTE MICHEAUX

© 2018 Dante Micheaux

Cover art: Jean-Baptiste Oudry, La Danse, c. 1720–1723.

Panel painted for Louis Fagon at the Château de Voré

Book design: Sophie Appel

Book editor: Sarah E. Bode

Published by Indolent Books,

an imprint of Indolent Arts Foundation, Inc.

www.indolentbooks.com

Brooklyn, New York

ISBN: 978-1-945023-20-0

καὶ μέν οἱ κῆρυξ ὀλίγον προγενέστερος αὐτοῦ
εἵπετο· καὶ τόν τοι μυθήσομαι, οἷος ἔην περ.
γυρὸς ἐν ὤμοισιν, μελανόχροος, οὐλοκάρηνος,
Εὐρυβάτης δ᾽ ὄνομ᾽ ἔσκε· τίεν δέ μιν ἔξοχον ἄλλων
ὧν ἑτάρων Ὀδυσεύς, ὅτι οἱ φρεσὶν ἄρτια ᾔδη.

༺༺༻

for Remica Bingham
sorella nel mestiere

CONTENTS

I

CENTER RING

5

II

FUNHOUSE

11

III

OUTSIDE, THE PROPHET

19

IV

DEATH OF THE CRACKHEAD VENDOR

25

V

STRIKING THE TENTS

29

Notes 35
Acknowledgments 41

CIRCUS

I

CENTER RING

All months are cruel, ladies and gentlemen.
The lilacs that last in the dooryard bloomed are dead,
so come you here for pleasure and we shall entertain.
See us Negroes dance and sing, dance and sing
for you, dear audience, we will do most anything.   5
Our jungle bunnies dance the cooch
for nickel, dime, anytime.
Big George can lift a heifer on his shoulder,
sip a brew and shine your shoe, but barely breaks a sweat.
Oh, and Trickster, in the stands   10
will borrow money, steal your wallets
and pay you back in advance.
Dangling Daniel hangs from a noose,
bug-eyed but do not fear.
For just one more dollar you can make him holler   15
with the crack of a whip in your hand.
Step right up! Encourage the kids.
Out back, there's a ninny parade.
Come one, come all; tell your friends!
This is the show that never ends…   20

Let's take a minute to thank all those
that brought and keep us here.
Up in the box is Mr. Washington Adams Jefferson,
decorated general, statesman, and agrarian.
Spotlight, please!   25

And to his left, Abimbola, the great tracker,
tamer of African wilds.
To his right is Mr. Nagrom, financier extraordinaire.
An appreciative round of applause for him!
Now if everyone would rise to their feet   30
to thank the one, without whom
none of this would be possible:
Miss Lily White, in whose honor we perform.

   Who talk like me? Who dye elect despise?
   Who patois, out day home, invite guffaw   35
   and swallow rage? Mask, except foe day eyes,
   who talk like me? Who dye elect despise?

Just call me Tom, the tallyman.
I keeps de Negroes in check;
they won't get far from me.   40
Enough of all this pomp; the circumstance is this:
with great big smiles and that old nigger shimmy,
we will give you laughs a-plenty.
But to begin this revelry,
we'll try a little mystery.   45
Aunt Cahrie, decrepit sage of the veil
will take her place and fix herself to see
the future, mister and mistress.
Not for me, but you and he—she
needs no sinister deck to be   50

the oracle of the street made black.
Here comes your fortune in a whisper:

"I see a great metropolis, yet hell is underneath;
because its populace has sinned,
the black rat is bequeathed.   55
They tunnel through the underworld
and nest inside the walls,
they nibble on the limbs of babes,
heed not the piper's call.
This plague, this pestilence you have?   60
You brought upon yourselves.
The lust it takes to own the world
is rooted deep and delves into abyss of hate—
that place you call your soul.
Your god is terribly displeased.   65
To expiate, and spare the rod,
live in the place where the black rat trod.
Become the rat itself."

I'm afraid the old auntie's tired now.

Fear the real city of the hag's vision   70
some other time. You're here to ease your guilt.
Neither bloody water, frogs, gnats, flies, diseased cattle,
boils, thunder and hail, locusts, darkness nor
the ghosts of dead sons will find you here.

Stay a while.   75
Gracious masters, you were not meant to fret.
There're those of us, as you know, more adept
at bearing burdens not our own.
So let us dance and sing for you.
As long as we dance and sing   80
there is nothing to forgive.
Whenever past atrocities begin to furrow your brow,
say this mantra: *mine is the peace of the world,*
the salvation of all within. I am the soil and the sky,
the beasts and superior kin. This is day that I have made;   85
this is the path that I have laid; I am the hope of the world.
Forgive this rape, la sottise, l'erreur, le péché, la lésine.

II

FUNHOUSE

Chipped brownstone stoops cradle the detritus of life.
She is one, lost in satiety, the bliss of oblivion,
harlot of the dope in her veins.   90
Behind her looms a hell
rich with the darkness of forgetting,
even in daylight, in view of children
taught to steer clear but never do, curious
about the freedom of barely clothed women   95
who do not work
and men with big cars
whose pockets are lined with money,
unlike their fathers—who *do* exist,
who conduct trains in the underworld,   100
who they never see,
who only see them when they are sleeping,
who know what they know about the world
but cannot protect them, who cannot rid their lives
of women like her, seen on the street everyday,   105
on the way to school, on the way home,
a face more familiar than their mother's,
with a name they remember
and include in rhyme.
She has asked them for a dollar before,   110
in the bodega next door to the house
on which stoop she sits,
its particleboard windows
keeping her shame

from the sight of passersby. 115
Inside, she is the plaything of Satan's doppelgangers,
the ball in a game of jacks, a hole-in-one,
her breasts like dice, her body
a crumpled lottery ticket
arching toward a nice shot. 120
Stumbling to the rhythm of no music, she laughs,
drools, knowing that at the end of this dance
she will be offered the favor she desires most,
the luster on her tongue,
the calm of fantastic stupor 125
in a corner, on a corner, cornered.
In such a state, she dreams
of ridiculous wealth by a pool, in a fur coat,
but wakes on a pile of dead rats,
phlegmatic, too gone to go. 130
She's hungry and can hear an ice cream truck
outside, makes for the door, makes for the curb
where the ice cream truck is, does not have a dollar.

You wanna taste my sweet sugar nasty, little boy?
You buy me a vanilla cone and you can have a taste. 135
You wanna little of this sugar nasty?
You buy me a ice cream cone, with sprinkles.
I bet you ain never had no sugar nasty.
How old you is? You bout old as my little boy.
Hey don't you want some this here here, 140

make a little man outta you, little boy?
Get me a ice cream cone, with sprinkles.
Say, little boy? You hear me talkin to you.
You wanna little of this sugar nasty?

Yeah, says a little boy, not so little as he is young,   145
sharp, aware of this house
he has passed each day of his life,
who knows this woman,
like everyone knows this woman,
as Adam knew Eve because he had no other choice.   150
He strikes a deal. *Yeah—and what about my friend?*
What you gone give him if he buy you a ice cream?
The friend smiles; it's funny.
They've bought her before, for less
but she doesn't remember; her kidneys lust   155
for the saccharine delight, which she will forget
in an instant. *Yeah, what I get? Freaky? Freaky?*
The people on the street watch this barter;
the adults comply.
Other children learn this madness,   160
cultivate it, come home late,
tell their mothers they were at play.
The mothers never ask at what? with whom?

She smiles and *sugar nasty* fails at seduction.
The boys have no idea what it is   165

and will never have to know
because it's the everyday alchemy,
the things that *stuff* will make women do
—of which they've heard their grandmothers,
surrogate mothers, aunts, the ladies at the bus stop speak. 170
But they know what a woman's insides feel like,
buy two ice cream cones with sprinkles
and follow her double-fisted, backward lure
into the condemned house of tricks and trade,
into a moribund world of creaky stairs, 175
sparse slivers of light,
bedless bedrooms and lecherous walls.
Here, the cat is always away.

Little boys like mystery;
they master the magic of curiosity 180
and wield it through what they discover:
orgy of vermin; sharp objects in the dark;
sounds they've heard coming
from their mother's bedroom
or muted on after-hours television; 185
living heat;
the smell of burning sugar;
the flash of gold teeth in the unknown;
gum on the floor and webs on the brow.
She keeps the promise of her *sweet sugar nasty* in the air 190
and the little boys' tummies begin to quiver;

they are fighting
the wrong-it's wrong-you know it's wrong feeling
(but will feel better afterwards, like conquerors,
like little men with mannish ways,   195
deserving of a pat on the shoulder, a smile from Dad
when, years from now, they tell the story),
the usual before one bares his sex.
She finds an empty niche, finishes what's left
of her payment and takes off her clothes.   200
Numb and spread-eagle on the floor, she invites
the boys with a sticky finger, one at a time,

                                        later together,
into to an unkempt and musky void.
They sink into her clutches, tighter than vise-grips,   205
with a clumsy start, all nerves and erection.
The pit is addictive and overwhelms, coaxes their spirits
from the inside out. Once entered, they can never leave,
the foolish prey of a monster.

III

OUTSIDE,
THE PROPHET

for Amiri Baraka

• • • woe unto you   illusionseekers   210
the milk from the breast
of the benevolent stepmother
is tainted with illusions
refuse   hold your breath, brethren
remember   on route to the land   215
of milk and honey   is the desert
and the milk is an illusion
and the honey is funnyhoney
acidhoney   tripyououthoney
the desert is where you want to be   220
stayway from the water
remember   where the water brought you
be rabid in the endless water
swallow and die
the illusions make you dance   225
slide   dip   shake   boogaloo
shangalang   aint no thang
but a chaingang
elude the illusions
the illusions want more   and then some   230
the illusions want work   (with no sass)
and entertainment
why you think you dancin'?
you on a partyride
it's shock   therapy   235
which causes dehydration

which causes want of water
why you think you dancing   (stayway from the water)
to a worthless thing?
the illusions are worthless   240
and you who follow illusion   become worthless
how empty your worship
in a godmade world
with your handmade apocalypse
and its denigrated singing   245
you have been given poisoned water to drink
and the thirst is an illusion   makes you dance
the spectators are impatient for popcorn
(for its salt   for your weight in salt)
          as they watch the show that never ends   250
and become thirsty   and drink the water
and become corrupted   by their own illusions
heed   dancers and singers in the machine
stop   and listen to the noise subside
and don't be surprised that you made the noise   255
or that the spectators are quiet   gone mute long ago
you crush the hearts and shake the bones of your prophets
and do not hear
become a menace to your enemies
cease praying to the gone   260
you have the proof   you are the proof
why you think you dancin'?
can't you feel it?   onetwostep

the exhaustion?   onetwostep
they love it when you onetwostep   265
why do you think you're dancing?
the weaker, the more you feel it
the slipshod guilt of a gyrating stripper
blind to redemption
a clutch of dollar bills in hand   270
there is remedy   a dose
to pry you free from sanity: the marvelous trick of illusion
stop dancing
stop singing
horde the (giving it up) treasure   275
you have forsaken your house
and abandoned your heritage
and given up your heart to its enemies
your eyes are false   diluted
your colors fade   280
you have become fat mimicries
slaves to the audience
a partyallthetime madness   bloated beyond belief
flee the Big Top
come into the sun   and be still   285
baptize in the light
be still   sweat
let it seep out you
        or have it beat out you

kill the honkey's monkey   or eternity awaits you   290
      in the Disco Inferno
you are weary from holding it in
take off your clothes   run naked
let it all hang loose if you feeling afflicted
these lords love a sinner   295
      shake what ya massa gave you
shake it loose
wrest yourselves from it
it's not yours   it never was
just part of the contract   part of the deed   300
became your creed
you have the proof   you are the proof
cease praying to the gone
become a menace to your enemies
stop the show   for none will bemoan you   305
      your yoke tossed off   and sinking in time
no buoy for those giddy   and drowning in the water
stayway from the water
remember   where the water brought you
swallow and die   310
the hour has already scattered   here
in the unreal city
heed   dancers and singers in the machine
you are its industry   crumble!
flee the Big Top   315

IV

DEATH OF
THE CRACKHEAD
VENDOR

Roany? That junkie's selling popcorn?
Moonlighting, must be. No more *cheap smokes.*
No more *six of anything you need for five dollars!*
The shop won't be the same without that Negro
     interrupting my haircut.
Poor Miss Deb somewhere drunk with grief.   320
With him, everything was for sale.
He was down on Front Street one time with his dick
     hanging out.
He ain't never had good sense, though wasn't his fault.
I knew for sure he was dead—in that alley, stone cold
as a black marble statue, sitting on a brand new A/C unit.   325

V

STRIKING
THE TENTS

Cartwheels and hallellujahs festoon the heat.
Underneath a white tarpaulin: holiness
in all its unholy rejoicing.

What once sheltered a boy's laughter
          comes down,   330
comes down on the heads of a people,
comes down on our heads and few notice.
The poles, the ropes, sink into the ground.
Pressed against the tarp there is no sound
but The Spirit makes the bodies writhe.   335

The old mothers offer their dwindling soprano,
a precious utterance that summons The Savior—
the only sound that summons these days, last days.
The old mothers know the end of days.
They sweat a passion in their white dresses   340
and kerchiefs, pray for strength and necessary talk.

    Satan, get thee behind me!

Who says from the pulpit I LOVE THE NAME!
but stretches out a hand to signal hats, chargers
and velvet bags with wooden handles?   345

    Pastor!

He getting ready to come down, you hear me?

    Pastor!

He getting ready to preach!

    Pastor!   350

He getting ready to sully all that Italian silk,
while we fan the flies in this cotton (we done picked) *field.*

What once sheltered a boy's curiosity
      comes down,
comes down in wails of fever pitch,   355
comes down in the grin of an ungodly charlatan
and few notice.

        SOME MAN, SOME WOMAN,
        SOME BOY, SOME GIRL?

More people or less room?   360
"Go on, baby, and receive
the right hand of fellowship."

Down by the river, under which I was put,
by my own accord, I asked in prayer,
in my silent time, in fear I asked.   365

The book read: after the water there is only life.
So, when I was bad, when it was a secret,
when I knew it was no mistake,
when I saw the blood moon
and crawled under the bed,   370
away from the avenging angels,
away from the blast of the horn,
before the earth shook and closed my eyes,
I asked for the water, asked to be taken,
to be put under, so far under, under death,   375
under sin, under the world of nights,
asked for the water and not the shadow dance
of the men behind the shades.

After the water was light.
After the light, there was clarity in waves.   380
After clarity, death remained and decision.

"Go on and receive the right hand of fellowship."
No.
Not yet.
Let them sing a little more about Yonder,   385
about the Upper Room, about glory.
I am not ready to step from the pews,
to make my way up the aisle,
in the eyes of the on-lookers.
I have been down by the river and was taken   390

by the water. "Accept his hand and see his face."
Then what would *you* do? I'd need no other guide.
The fellowship offered is not clarity.
A body still clings to the polymeric cross,
      bound by neon lights   395
but this body, the dark meat of God's great chicken,
awaits the good news, the gospel of bread and butter.

One by one, the congregants proclaim
themselves sinners by leaping into the air.
Cleanse me, Lord! They join the waiting   400
to be touched by the revivalist, to feel
the charisma move through him as he grasps
neck and brow, holding their head—
a crystal ball in a clairvoyant's hands.

      HEALING! HEALING!   405

His gratitude for whatever private anguish
has brought our people low.

If I pray the kingdom down to here and now,
the Lord will reveal me.

      HEALING! HEALING!   410
      I ASK FOR A HEALING MIRACLE
      NOW! THAT SHE BE HEALED

FROM THE CROWN OF HER HEAD
TO THE SOLES OF HER FEET.
BE HEALED! BE MADE WHOLE!   415
PEOPLE RAISE YOUR HANDS!
GET YOUR HEALING RIGHT NOW!

A strange and glorious feeling came over my body.
This is how it ends,
in sudorific showmanship,   420
the noise of tamborines
and speaking in tounges,
ushers and nurses, of the church,
choreographed to catch the fainting,
the fallen, whipped into perfect distraction   425
by the matchless name of Jesus,
as tithes and offerings are loaded
into the trunk of a car
and the old mothers, BLESS THEIR SOULS,
rake out our sustenance   430
into aluminum garbage cans.

    Amen. Selah! Amen.

NOTES

Not only the title, but the plan and a good deal of the signi-
fying of the poem were suggested by Mr. Ralph Ellison, Jr.'s
inscription that the "path of [my] song is uppity like the sun."
Indeed, so deeply am I indebted, Mr. Ellison's negritude will
elucidate the difficulties of the poem much better than my
notes can do; I recommend it (apart from the great interest in
the quality or fact itself) to any who thinks such elucidation of
the poem worth the trouble. To another text I am indebted in
general, one which should have influenced a generation pro-
foundly; I mean *Harlem Gallery*; I have used especially three
cantos: *Alpha*, *Delta*, and *Omega*. Anyone who is acquainted
with these works will immediately recognize in the poem cer-
tain references to shit-talking occasions.

I. CENTER RING

Line 1. Cf. Eliot, *The Waste Land* I, i.

2. Cf. Whitman, "When Lilacs Last in the Dooryard
   Bloom'd."

34–37. V. Nelson, "Triolets for Triolet."

38. Cf. Whitman, "The Indications."

46. Matriarch of the notorious Melbournes of Trenton, New Jersey.

51. Cf. Palcy/Truffaut, *La Rue Cases-Nègres* (1983).

58. Cf. Wette, *Hänsel und Gretel*.

72–74. Cf. Exodus VII, xiv–XI, vi; XII, xxix.

87. Cf. Baudelaire, "Au Lecteur," verse 1.

II. FUNHOUSE

Part II, as a whole, is derived from the tone set by Toni Morrison, specifically, through the character of Ruth Foster Dead in *Song of Solomon*—which can also be found in her novels, from *The Bluest Eye* to *A Mercy*.

205. Cf. "How We Do" (Trina, featuring Fabolous), verse 50.

208. Cf. "Hotel California" (The Eagles), verse 40.

III. OUTSIDE, THE PROPHET

Amiri Baraka (1934–2014) was the umpteenth reincarnation of Anansi and an avatar of the Trickster God. He was last revealed to me on the morning of October 7, 2012, across the breakfast table at 17-18 Upper Woburn Place and later that night, with celebratory dark rum, at 3 Varnishers Yard.

215. Cf. Exodus, III, viii.

223. Cf. Hurston, *Their Eyes Were Watching God*: "Dat water is somethin' wrong wid it. It nelly choke me tuh death."

234. Cf. "Electric Boogie" (Marcia Griffiths), verse 21.

250. Cf. "The Song That Doesn't End" (Norman Martin), verse 1.

257. Cf. Jeremiah, XXIII, ix.

259. Cf. Jordan, "I Must Become A Menace to My Enemies."

261. V. Denzel Washington.

263–265. Cf. "1, 2 Step" (Ciara, featuring Missy Elliot), verse 12.

289. Cf. Meyjes, *The Color Purple* (1985): "I know what it like wanna sing and have it beat out 'ya."

294. V. "Intro" (Da Brat, featuring Millie Jackson), verse 7.

295. Cf. "Round About De Mountain" (Florence Quivar), verse 5.

305. Cf. Jeremiah XV, v.

315. Cf. Reubens/McGrath, *Big Top Pee-Wee* (1988).

IV. DEATH OF THE CRACKHEAD VENDOR

316. Grandson of the matriarch of the notorious Melbournes of Trenton, New Jersey.

320. Mother of the Crackhead Vendor and eldest daughter of the aforementioned matriarch.

V. STRIKING THE TENTS

327–328. Cf. Hill, "Psalms of Assize."

347. V. my maternal grandmother (1930–2012).

349. Ibidem.

358–359. V. the Reverend Doctor T. L. Steele.

361–362. V. my maternal grandmother (1930–2012).

363. Cf. Villanueva, "As the river crests, mud-rich with forgotten things."

369. Cf. Green/Green, *The Seventh Seal* (1988).

385. Cf. "Goin' Up Yonder" (Tramaine Hawkins).

386. Cf. "In the Upper Room" (Mahalia Jackson).

396. Cf. Robinson, *Amazing Grace* (1974).

397. V. Carpenter, *My Days and Dreams*.

405. V. A. A. Allen.

426. Cf. the Reverend Linda Tarry-Chard.

ACKNOWLEDGMENTS

Margo Berdeshevsky for the grand errand.

Dr. Antony Makrinos, University College London, for sharing his knowledge and extending his patience.

Matteo Campagnoli for linguistic affirmation.

Jumoké Fashola, broadcast journalist and vocalist, for the invitation. This poem was first read in its entirety to a public audience on March 27, 2017, at Hoxton Hall, London.

"Circus" first appeared in *What Rough Beast*—an online poetry series published by Indolent Books.

ABOUT THE AUTHOR

Dante Micheaux is the author of *Amorous Shepherd* (Sheep Meadow Press, 2010). His poems and translations have appeared in *Poetry, The American Poetry Review, Callaloo, PN Review, The African American Review* and *Tongue*—among other journals and anthologies. He has been shortlisted for the Benjamin Zephaniah Poetry Prize and the Bridport Prize. Micheaux's honors include a prize in poetry from the Vera List Center for Art & Politics, the Oscar Wilde Award and fellowships from Cave Canem Foundation and The New York Times Foundation.

ABOUT INDOLENT BOOKS

Indolent Books is a small nonprofit poetry press founded in 2015 and operating in Brooklyn, N.Y. Indolent publishes poetry by underrepresented voices whose work is innovative, provocative, and risky, and that uses all the resources of poetry to address urgent racial, social, and economic justice issues and themes.

Web: indolentbooks.com
Instagram: @indolent_books
Twitter: @IndolentBooks

CPSIA information can be obtained
at www.ICGtesting.com
Printed in the USA
BVHW090123041218
534641BV00027B/1585/P

9 781945 023200